JN440343

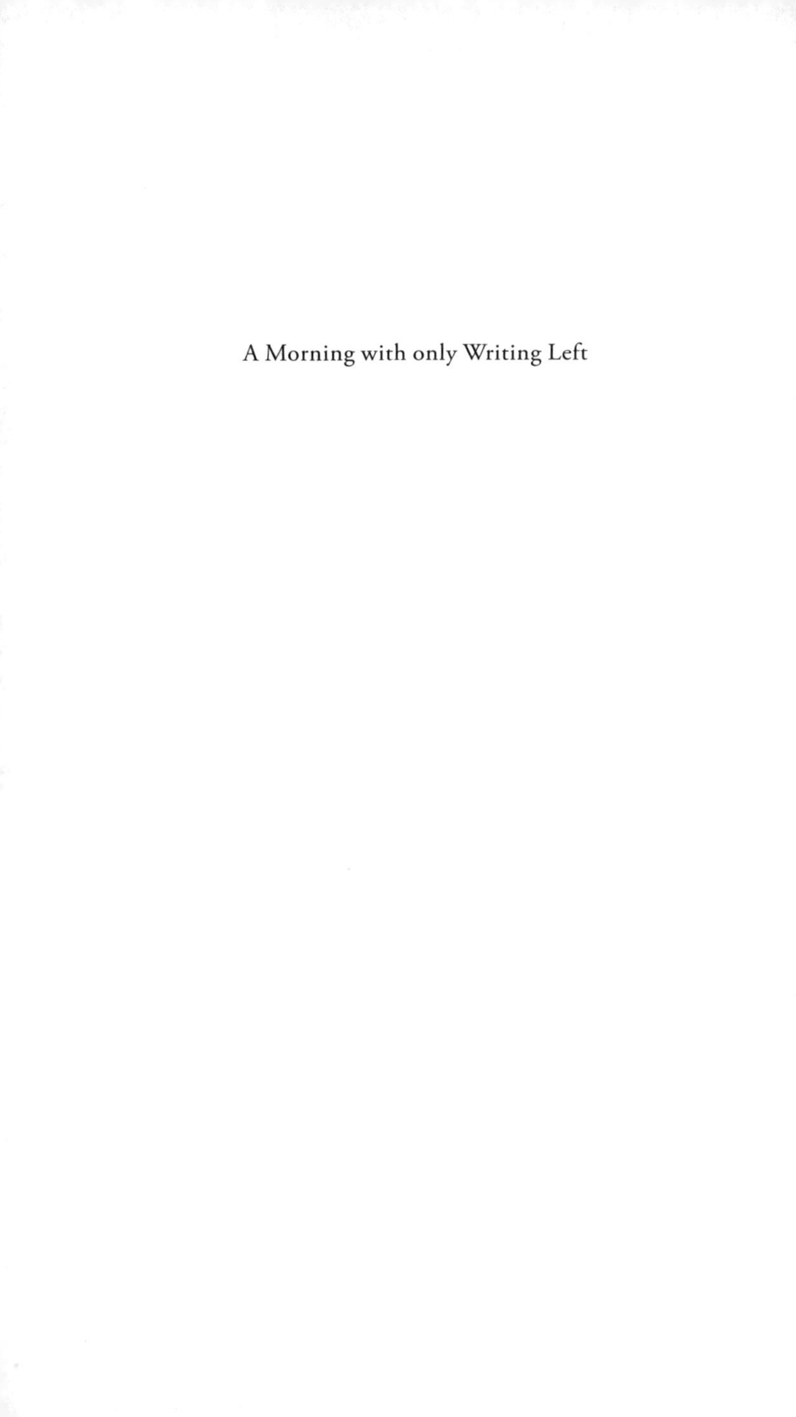

A Morning with only Writing Left

A Morning with only Writing Left

A collection of new poems by Park Jang-ho
Translated by Brother Anthony of Taizé

K POET

아시아

Contents

Wolf's teeth left in a notebook 9

Even if it's an unbearable face,
even if it's a love I'll lose again 15

The sound of a wolf's teeth calling 18

Facial expressions at the speed of light 27

Light with a distorted expression 30

A morning with only letters left 31

Ignorance 42

The doll cried without waking up 45

Ho—Counterattack of deleted files 48

Book of time covered in an epidermis 51

Swarming Ho's 59

Return certificate for overdue time 67

Smooth as a straight line 75

Marine Snow 79

I cried like a river 84

Impossible Ho 85

We cut our nails together 89

Potato growing thick 92

Hello melanin 95

Harmonious flowers 100

Poet's Note 106

Poet's Essay 110

Commentary 120

What They Say About t Park Jang-ho 130

A MORNING WITH ONLY WRITING LEFT

Wolf's teeth left in a notebook

I opened my newly bought notebook. The blank space of the unlined pages is a snowfield covered with early snow. Taking the first step is difficult. Only a cruel heart that tramples on clean things can write the first phrase. I sense a sentence flickering on the paper. It is written in invisible ink. Traces that visible when you close your eyes and disappear when you open your eyes. Traces of the wrist.

Speaking of cruelty, I once drew on my wrist a line that wasn't in any notebook. What I wanted to trample on was tedium. Traces like handcuffs that fit snugly on the wrist. In the truth games of later fakes, I hoped that everyone would believe the memories I brought out. There is only one truth. Either one of my fingers that counted lies wasn't mine, or only one was mine. The melancholy that couldn't be chosen, rolling and rolling, transformed into a snowman, hidden in an empty glass.

I see the white wrists freed of handcuffs. I look at the notebook waiting for a sentence. Why is the inside of the notebook mostly white? Why does snow fall inside my body when I see something white? There were winters when there was no snow, but when I open a new notebook, it is always a snowfield. White snow piles up softly on my wrists.

The child kept glancing towards the old castle as it waited for you. If it's wrinkled and skinny, eyes drawn by the child will sprout on my forearm. The old castle rises tall at the end of a distant tattoo. Is there still a vassal child playing alone waiting for the king? You didn't come until I closed my eyes. Your love is a plant in a wine glass. When the plant withered, you were reticent toward me. Like you, I also love myself as a plant in a wine glass. The plant grows thick. The plant grows thick. Even if the glass dries up, I must not wither. And I have to yearn again. Since I only looked like you.

A flash of light gleamed from inside the paper. It's the gaze of an old wolf that hunts memories! I bought a recycled paper notebook! Can anyone say that yellow that looks white is yellow? Opening the unspeakable yellow, what am I recycling? Opening my eyes to disappearing things shall I recycle faceless first love with the qualification of a love that can only be obtained by closing my eyes?

A sad deer

You were a deer,

a peerless deer only glimpsed from behind

A heart unable to speak becomes a wolf.

At night, a wolf's howling could be heard

coming from the notebook at my bedside.

Even if I opened it, only that sound could be heard.

The notebook had snowfields vaster than the number of pages.

For the wolf howling in hiding

I wrote a deer.

For the illiterate wolf

I also drew a fat deer.

Mornings when the picture was eaten

and only the letters remained

were always sad.

Expressing it in the form of a recollection, my love in love with sorrow was cowardly and being cowardly was more tedious than being sad, so I chewed the wine glass and opened the first page of my notebook. Nothing is as difficult as the first time.

Trampling with a cruel heart on the emptiness, I wrote this first chapter. The wolf's teeth were left in tatters in the notebook.

Even if it's an unbearable face,
even if it's a love I'll lose again

Wolves teeth were left that had to be read in the morning.
It was a sign of a love that couldn't bear people.
In a morning after a sleepless night, there is no distinction between yesterday and today
and an undivided sound erased the difference between me and the wolf.
I transplanted my face to match my teeth
and brushed my teeth from wolf to human.
Everything that has disappeared is considered dead.
Yes, everything that has disappeared is dead.
The toothless wolf mades a whistling sound
and chose a place to lie down on the snowy field outside my notebook.

We have to live somehow,

a life after death.

Even if it's not true that we are reborn

if we don't die, we can't even expect it.

Because something has been lost, something can be found.

You lose people while I lose love.

Let's survive, let's live, even if it's false that we became one face.

Let's start with a sound, a sound of writing on paper.

Wolves teeth left to be read in the morning.

How long have you been trapped in this sentence that almost turned into a tragedy?

There were no fixed letters, so I survived by eating

only what was erased.

Have I become accustomed to the habit of erasing because there is nothing that has to exist?

For now I can eat anything that has become writing.

Even if it's an unbearable face, even if it's a love I'll lose again,

We are no longer sad. Are not cowardly.

A welcome, bright morning has come like a sentence from the end of the world.

The sound of a wolf's teeth calling

This notebook has a title.
Large gothic print occupies the center of the cover
and unreadable letters the size of sesame seeds
are spread beneath the title.
Countless sentences that exist but have no meaning
float above the title to the top.
It looks like something I've seen a lot somewhere.
I open the cover and enter the notebook.
The first page is torn out.
He said those things were wolf's teeth left in the notebook.
That's the first sentence in this notebook.
What had he plucked out so that the remaining teeth were so sharp?

What was he going to write that made him tear out what he had written?

Do you want to stop wondering about unanswered questions?

I've entered the notebook, but I haven't said anything yet.

"Wolf's teeth left that I have to read in the morning."

This is not what I said. That's what he said.

He's out of the notebook.

Things that were born, but don't exist.

I think I've been through it a few times.

I feel the irresponsibility of an unlicensed surgeon

who sewed up with thread a soldier's leg

which a bullet had penetrated, then sent him back

to the battlefield.

The condition for an incompetent person to feel proud is irresponsibility.

The wolf's teeth call the sound,
call the sound inside me.
We have to believe in the field and the status quo.
We have to trust the local topography and the rotting legs of soldiers.
We have to admit how close to death
are maggots that come out alive through the skin.
I'll call that sound into the wolf's teeth.
Traces of vowels remain on the teeth.
The vowel is the sound of a beast that creeps on all fours.
The problem is that I have too many beasts.

Some sounds make me sick and some make me excited.

It's not the sound that moves me. The sound guides me.

I need a good sound rather than a good meaning.

I want to walk with the right handwriting as much as a good sound.

I'll have to change what he said a little when he starts walking.

"It's a morning when you have to read a wolf with only teeth left."

Since the writing is being ripped out, reading can become writing.

Wolf, let us write a poem long enough not to forget the title.

According to déjà vu, organic sentences can be continued indefinitely, but

I can't deal with the missing pages.

I don't even know why I've entered the notebook.

Let's not stop walking even if meaningless sentences are jumbled up.

Just as I was not born to live, but live because I was born,

I don't need blank space to write, I need writing to fill the blank space.

Writing rather than things written,

writing like breathing, writing like eating,

writing like working, writing like playing,

writing like resting, writing like sleeping,

thus, writing like living, finally, writing like dying.

I don't only have good sounds

but look at the lawlessness rampant outside the notebook.

A sound is okay. In this notebook

no one gets scammed, no one gets beaten up, no one gets killed.

There's no need to blame yourself if the handwriting looks like this.

For it seems the cover of this notebook won't open.

How did the writing teacher teach the world's bad handwriting?

It was like the cosmos not leering.

Gathering, exploding and scattering,

teeth remain in the notebook, and writing remains with me.

There's a future no one knows about in this notebook.

I have a notebook that no one will open in that future.

The notebook has a future that no one knows about.

I have a notebook that no one will open in that future.

With my handwriting, I can't play an adult role at all.

Even if a sentence that came too quickly from the future mocks me,

like electricity that finds its own wire

no matter how many wires are twisted together,

let's go through all the blank spaces in front of the teeth as if it were my way.

The title is what happens outside the notebook.

Let me try to run smoothly in the notebook.

I understand the poet who wrote only one line of poetry in ten years,

Taking his prudence, his seriousness, and his incompetence

as my irresponsible favoritism, having sworn to live with only one person.

Putting the title decided outside,

let's pull out a very long stitch even if it looks like it's going to break,

like a maggot that randomly tears the skin here and there

Hey Mr. Doctor, I'll be able to walk again, right?

He said, I'm sorry, but it's not my responsibility.

Because there were not enough doctors back then!

Facial expressions at the speed of light

The title of this notebook is 'I am the Light'. The title written on the cover is surrounded by tiny letters small as sesame seeds. On some days the unreadable text seems to escort the title and on other days to enclose the title. On another day like today, the letters are staging a cover war. They awaken my past, that I had forgotten or pretended to have forgotten. A civil war in the body where hormonal shells were rampant. The flowers that bloomed through my face, flowers of red pus all over it. I was reborn with the scars of the flowers that were cut out. As I lost love, sorrow also disappeared.

I diverge from the letters' battlefield, where it is impossible to distinguish which is the defending army and which the encircling army, and enter the notebook. I look at the wolf's teeth with a face that has lost its original form. Wolf, you are not the light. You are the child of a torn sound. From the beginning, your sorrow which has quit the title has no face and my face has no sorrow, so let's become one.

I think of myself as you, like a beast that is so hungry that it devours its own flesh. I think of people as me. I think of bad people as people. I think of bad things as bad people. My memories holding only bad things are Hell. In order not to be discovered by the title, I dig a hole in the page and bury Hell in the smallest letters I can write. When I close the notebook, the cover is today and another day. Does the title command or defend what is written? I feel a sad sentence falling at the speed of light in search of a face to stay in with the gravity of a mind that couldn't overcome the cliff.

Light with a distorted expression

Born on the cover as a title without any content,
I wait for content to come out.
surrounded by unreadable letters,
When I hear the sound and enter the notebook,
when I return to the cover
as if reflected in the mirror of my private life
that unfolds independently of me,
the difficulty of the more prominent letters
is such that I don't know what they're saying to me
and the light that collapses into the handwriting hurts my heart,
the twinkling light of tears.

A morning with only letters left

I have a pen I want to throw away. I am holding that pen right now. The pen stand is transparent, so the inside can be seen clearly. It's almost out of ink. I scribble a line on scrap paper. Cross it out. I feel like a person who is alive and not dead even though the time to die of old age has passed because of the energy that was not used when it should have been used. This pen is a fountain pen. But it is disposable. It's funny to say that it's a disposable fountain pen, and when I hold it in my hand it's creepy like my only life. Now I want to send you this pen. I open the notebook and send the pen as the hand pleases.

Whether it's a book or a movie, from start to finish

I guess I'll have to watch it at least twice.
But you I can only see once.
The unknown fact of a human being sad because
it's only once.
I won't get drunk.
I'll look at you soberly
Even with a difficult work
that I can't understand, but I can appreciate.

When the devil is busy, instead of himself
he sends you a drink.
The third party is now gone.
Go tell the devil
that if he wants to ruin me, he'll have to come

himself.

Sprawling. The nib scratches the paper. It seems to be tearing the skin of time. I have the illusion that it is not the ink that is running, but the paper bleeding. Paper has a past. The past of paper is plants. A single sentence-flower blooms on a plant.

"You look more cheerful when we break up than when we meet."

I have a past too. Flowers revealed my past. My past is a monster. I was pierced by a thorn while trying to pick the flower. A sentence of two flowers is written on the finger.

"We won't break up anymore.

You will only break up with me again."

The devil has come. The devil conducts an existence experiment. "Will it be brighter when you break up with yourself than when you meet?" Even demons have different abilities. Existence. Lyricism. Experiment. Training. Lyrical experimentation and practice of existence. A lyrical practice of experimental existence. Experimental practice of lyrical existence. Experimental lyricism of a practicing being. I add words and change the word order to deceive the devil. I learned more about myself than the devil. My practice outstrips the devil's experiment. I won't be experimented on. I won't be broken. I will not be abandoned. To the devil, I am the devil. I will test the devil with practice. The experiment will fail and the devil will be thrown out of the lab.

Do you know why humans can't fly?
Because they are not sure they can fly.
If you don't believe it, stand on the cliff.
You can only fly if you have 100% certainty.
Can you fly?

When you stretch out your arms in front of you, your palms
become the ceiling of a bottomless cave.
Of the words hanging there, only the certain ones
will fly to poetry.
If nothing flies, a fall of words without content,

their grip exhausted. will be seen.

I change the page. Dog-eared. A blank page with the wind turning the corners. This is a dog's inner ear. The wind has read the nature of the blank space that has not yet been written on and can be used for anything. Morning releases an apple here. I slice the apple with a knife. A substance that disappears at the same time as the skin is peeled off. The reason I stayed silent for a while after finishing with the knife was because I wanted the deep meaning of the lost apple. I erase the meaning which crumples on being laid aside and release a sound into the morning. Words without content glide through bottomless white space. A word calls discarded words and leads them to a sentence. A sentence calls discarded sentences and leads them into a paragraph. The sound of a paragraph destined to be discarded also crumples with its own meaning, and you unfold it. The more it is unfolded, the more the meaning becomes crumpled. Then I'll lay it out first. Just crumple it. The wrinkles expand. The expansion crumples.

The moment you write on paper, there is another side. While I live, the other side of life arises. I fill in the other side of life with the inside to create a surface. When the wind blows, the front and back sides fly together, and the birth that begins with death is read. Death is read from birth. The moment it is read, another side arises and expands.

Expands endlessly.

My waist is a stem,
growth is a rose that flees from its thorns,
no expression on my face,
sorrow is the snake's waist hidden in its long body
the snake crawls and leaps in the opposite direction to the rose,
holding in its teeth a thorn of the rose it swallowed,
it bites its tail and becomes a symbol.
Within it
the storm that sent the world flying is crying with nowhere to go.
Expansion of the symbols that overflow to the

other side of the crying

I needed a stage, so I put a frying pan on the gas stove. This stage is the other side of the inside. I crack the crying storm with an egg inside the bowl and add chopped onions and carrots, season with salt and stir. Light the fire and put in cooking oil. Sizzle. A crying yellow storm fills the stage. The I of life asks why I keep frying poems I can't even eat. The I of the other side answers. Now it's time for the poem to leave the paper. The inner self asks why I keep reading a blank notebook. The surface I answers. If you draw an underline, important sentences are written over it. Dog-eared. White paper folding in the wind. This is the inside of an empty dog's ear. Soon, something important will unfold within it. The other side of us that cannot be seen, no matter how much we live.

I had a pen I wanted to throw away. The pen was thrown away in the middle. Since then, this text has been written with a different pen. I die faster than you. No one can replace me. So please. Let me live longer than you. The unknown of a person sad because they're only once. There are flowers that smell only as they fall from the tree. That is you. After the day when I was only going to break up with myself, my heart calls for things.

Lily! Lily!

Just as your flowerpot was not sad
when you died after one day by my side,
Please disguise my morning misery
with those bright teeth.

He puts a knife on the smiling devil's forehead and shuts the notebook.

Ignorance

The letters uncoil.

They come crawling with my teeth left in the notebook.

My teeth are the beginning of this notebook.

Just as there seemed to be a double line that was ignored and passed,

just as it seems that if they begin again, they can become better writing,

the snakes are returning to the beginning.

But my teeth are turning into dogs' teeth.

Someone is taming me.

The beginning of the notebook is changing.

Even though I go back, I can't find the original starting point.

The path of infinity is another future of this note-book

Smile, snakes!

I'll put flowers in your hair.

Love, that reckless, fictional symbol.

—Where is this?

—We're almost there. Just a little further.

—Then, let's not spare the joy of our rehabilitation.

Snakes passing by dogs' teeth

whistle

Underline respectfully their instrumental ignorance!

The doll cried without waking up

The guests asked me to read a book. When I said "Jungle Book," they complimented me, saying how well I did it. Then they turned over the cover and opened the next page, waiting for me to go on reading. I couldn't read any other letters except 'Jungle Book'. Just as a pencil is a pencil and an eraser is an eraser, "Jungle Book" was an object, not letters, to me. I had no idea what "Jungle" was, what "Book" was, or why the child depicted inside the book was wandering around the forest naked. The guests shut their mouths because of my illiteracy and went out to the yard to make a fire. They were talking adult words that I could hear but not understand. I took the Jungle Book and went up to the attic. The children from other houses grew up as fast as beasts. In the attic were the books those children had handed down, and a Barbie doll with a broken neck. I laid out books, piled them up, opened them, used them to build a house, lay down in the book house and touched the doll. At that moment, a snake descended from the ceiling of the Jungle Book, crawled down the wall and grabbed the doll. I chased the snake into the book and met an unknown wolf, an unknown leopard, an unknown bear, and an unknown tiger. When I asked where my sick doll was, they didn't answer anything. They told me to speak in writing. I stumbled and wrote Jungle Book a few times, then gave up and sat on a towering sentence* and looked out of the book. Not a single trace of barbarism remained in the yard that the civilized people had left. You came up into the attic and called my name, but I had disappeared into the Jungle Book. As swarms of wild monkeys ravaged the ruins of the city, you shattered the book house and, rising like dust from a demolition site, I healed my broken fingers. The sound of rats running over the attic ceiling was swift, and the doll cried without waking up.

* "First, I was turned away for being a man, and now, I'm being turned away for being a wolf. Let's go, Akela,"

Ho

—Counterattack of deleted files

We are the files Ho deleted,
the files mercilessly deleted without even being printed.
Ho is the ruling party of this body.
What was Ho's task as the party in power?
It was an excess of ideas and memos that couldn't even be used.
Why should we, who are innocent, be erased?
Why should we be abandoned without a name?
Look. I have no legs and you have no arms.
You have no eyes and you have no neck.
Some people have clogged nostrils and others have stuck lips.
Why do we have to die like this before we can live?

Ho must be replaced.
We must work together,
fill in the missing legs with the remaining legs,
align the remaining fists and the remaining el-
bows,
bite the lips to make the blood circulate,
even if we become Siamese twins with one shoul-
der,
even if we become myriapods with one ass,
we have to rise up,
we must rise up and gather,
we must come together and become an army.
Let's train,
luring with metaphors and symbols,
concealing with omissions and connotations,

guerrilla warfare disturbing with paradox and irony is also good.
Let's invent all kinds of strategies and tactics.
Let's use all kinds of tricks.
In "Smart bamboos grow in swimming pools"
guns and bayonets and grenades.
In "The flight of a butterfly carrying flames"
artillery, tanks, and fighters.
Let's open the door of blocked words and sentences and fill them with weapons.
Let's say the title is 'Ho'.
Ho is our enemy,
the enemy that drove us to death in deformity.
Let's infiltrate towards the title.
Let's get rid of Ho and make a new body.

Book of time covered in an epidermis

1.

It was the street going from Hongdae to Hapjeong. It was a raw fish place and there was party. Of the five people, only I wore glasses, and I was the only one of the opposite sex. My companions only ate the snacks while I drank alcohol. I went out to smoke a cigarette to calm my distant heart. It was before I even got drunk. A street tree struck my eye. It was wearing glasses without any lenses, with the same leopard-patterned frames as mine. Someone once asked: "If a shadow passes by the window of your room on a deserted island, what do you think it is?" A branch." "Then you were a tree in a previous life." The glasses seemed to prove it. I felt a sense of identity with the tree. It was like a human tree. I approached the tree and said hello. “Hello Mr. Tree.” The tree that I had greeted opened its eyes. Its eyes twinkled. Inside them, a leopard roared. It jumped into my eyes and drove my leopard away. The leopard from the tree standing by the roadside and my leopard coming out. My soul and the soul of the tree were swapped. Therefore, from now on, I was a tree that had become human. I finished smoking and went inside. It was a raw fish place and there was a party in progress. Don’t call me Mister. I sat there quietly and hung out with my friends. It was my first time but it was fun. Once the towering loneliness tall was gone, I finally got drunk. “Don’t blame me for being like a silent tree." "He's not to be blamed." I didn't feel any sense of alienation at all until the end of the party. I came out of the sushi restaurant and approached the tree to say goodbye. "Goodbye Mr. Tree." The group of people around me asked. "You seem to know this tree very well?" "It is a tree that cannot be called a stranger." I put my glasses back on and from Hapjeong headed for Hongdae to continue the party.

2.

I was a human being. No one loved me. I was punished for loving only myself They said I would turn into a tree. They said I would live as a tree until someone talked to me. I ran away My arms turned into branches, my lips into leaves, my face and body into trunks, and my legs into roots. No use, people only want to love people, it doesn't matter if it's me or someone else. A long time passed. Suddenly, I heard a voice: "Hello Mr. Tree." My eyes opened. A man with glasses was standing smoking. The frames of his glasses were the same leopard print as mine. The opportunity had come. An angry beast drove out a lonely beast and took over the man. My soul and his soul were exchanged. Therefore, from now on, I am a person who has become a tree. I know though my eyes were shut. You were not a tree turned into a human, but a person who was turning into a tree.

Only the glasses were left. I was a woman who only loved you and was afraid of breaking up. He went back into the restaurant then came out to say goodbye. "Goodbye, Mr. Tree." The man is leaving, leaving behind a tree that cannot be called a person. Watching his retreating back, I remembered the end of a conversation I once had with someone. "Why do you think those branches shook?" "A bird that was sitting there flew away." "You will only love what is flying away." The distance seemed to prove it. Someone who cannot be called a tree is moving away. I reached out towards him as he walked away. The more I loved, the more my arms were tangled in the sky. Good bye, man. All that is left of you as human, I will make disappear. You can keep alive with the men I have left. You will no longer be turning into a tree. As long as a person lives as a person, it doesn't matter if it's a man or a woman. Goodbye, human. Goodbye.

3.

Rhodopsin has disintegrated. A world that had been covered in darkness is revealed. Trees stood as trees, and people receded as people. Here is a land of paradoxes where blood vessels and vascular bundles are connected. A page of superstitions where conversation becomes a true story. When a tree blooms, a person's story begins. When a person's story ends, the tree loses its leaves. Each death becomes a shining star, and distant death, unsynchronized in the sky, blooms as a rose on a leopard's skin. We met in the story of the night. I close my eyes and think about the beginning of a conversation. "If you had a deep dream that you can't remember, where do you think it would be?" "An uninhabited island." "You want to live on a deserted island. But it's not an island in a dream. There is no one at your side." I opened my eyes Rhodopsin had disintegrated. He wasn't there and the candle was weeping alone. I missed him who had disappeared. Time transitioned into a story, and I saw the shadow of a moving tree outside the window and the feathers of a bird flapping its wings and flying from a branch. It was the eyes of the leopard that saw the bird leave the world of the inner skin holding in its beak the story it had shared with a candle. People are lonely because they have those eyes. The reason why a tree falls in love is because of the scent of roses that revolves around its body. A morning of the epidermis, where one and two leopards change places and move away. The book of time containing all those stories.

Swarming Ho's

An old wooden boat is drawn along by a scent of cherry blossom.

People wake up and have a drinking party on board.

'Hun' took control of the table, wiping away the dust that had accumulated on his eyelids.

A lip captain that flies away when called and builds up when left alone.

The moment I decided to depict his words

the name troubled me.

Hun was a name that 'Jeong' had worked out

so I deleted Hun because I wanted to write under a different name.

After I deleted it, I couldn't think of a new name.

Hun is Hun. I wanted to erase the Jeong who preempted Hun.
Just as I had decided to write about Hun and had deleted Hun's name
if I decided to write about Jeong, it seemed that I would have an excuse to erase Jeong.

'Jeong' is the one who unbuttons his shirt and fills the cup.
He is the thigh captain who speaks with his body.
The moment I decided to portray him
the name Jeong troubled me.
Jung was a name 'Kwon' had already copied
so that I wanted to delete Kwon, too.
He is the shadow captain who follows uncondi-

tionally

so if I wanted to erase him, I would have to describe him.

The name Kwon with nothing to describe was already used by 'X'.

So I wanted to delete Ho too.

Who Ho is I do not know.

I know no poems about Ho.

What is unknown can be filled in with what is known.

Ho was the Ho who brushed the dust off his eyelids and took control of the table.

Ho was the Ho who followed the Ho who took control of the table

Ho was the empty Ho who copied Ho and looked for liquor.

Ho, who rubbed the glass with his palm until sparks flew.

Ho who read poetry written with damp sparks.

Ho who earned the respect of chairs.

I met him nine times.

All that time he has never once seen me.

I know him and he doesn't know me.

He asked, pouring liquor into my glass,

Who are you?

Ho who keeps asking about the name he asked about.

Ho who keeps urging me to drink.
Ho who keeps reading the poem he read.
Ho who keeps dropping the dropped anchor.

I am a sailor on your ship. A janitor who cleans the deck.

His fire passed over into my drink.
He made me sing.
I sang burning lyrics.
The chairs that applauded me
Everything that was engulfed in flames in that moment was Ho.
Ho is a master at digging, a genius at sticking, and a master at sucking.

I wanted to erase Ho.

I wanted to put out Ho's fire that had taken hold of me.

Replacing the unknown with the known

I am continuing the poem about Ho.

Ho does not know Ho

so Ho cannot erase Ho.

So I have to finish writing a poem about him.

Hun, Jeong, and Kwon are different people.

Hun is the captain of an old wooden boat who wiped the dust on his eyelids and took control of the table.

Jeong is the captain of an old wooden boat who unbuttons his shirt and ignites a liquor glass.

Kwon is the captain of an old wooden boat who burns up time.

Ho that I can't see,
Ho that only I can hear well,
Ho who has no poem about him,
so I'm writing a poem about him.

Hun, Jeong, and Kwon were too old.
I'm singing the old names of people I've erased.
I write them, I throw them away
But this is a poem about Ho.
Hun, Jeong, and Kwon are Ho's erased poems.

They are Ho's poems restored to Ho.

He shakes his body as he swallows the burning liquor.

I can't erase Ho.

He has been alive for too long.

Return certificate for overdue time

I have lived half in the 20th century and half in the 21st century.
I haven't met contemporaries in a long time.

I wasn't depressed.
I just liked the word 'depressed'.
I liked the word, but I was sick with the meaning.
Maybe that was love.

Now is the time for ventilation to prevent infectious diseases!
Please open the window.

One disease presses one disease.

You, who I finally meet after a long while, are living far ahead.
After returning to live, I play all day long.
Even if I don't know how I survive, I know how you work.
I understand that work is survival.

On days when it's hard to sneeze because the assault on your eyes stings
grab my tickling nose and go home

Green sofa, comfy bed, burning flame,
objects that return first restore their function.

But the grandfather clock. I have a grandfather

clock, a friend gave it to me, the pendulum moves fast, but the hands have stopped. We are still boys of the 20th century. Sentences pushed to a still point of time pour out. This could be friendship. If the sentences are dense, the gravity will increase, and the there without us will be dragged here and will interfere with our privacy. But this moment was short-lived. We have to play without return. There is no floor here, and your silence and blank spaces as you work are being cited. By eating the out-pouring sentences, you become an even more perfect space between lines.

82 days of no-drinking and no-smoking.
I'm not depressed.

I just liked the word 'depressed'.

The voice of depression is as deep as a well.
There is still a 20th century boy in the well
egoism is getting more and more lonely.
Your dimples are rotting in your cheeks.
I feel lonely because there are no contemporaries around.

There is a high probability that future 'we' will grow farther away.
There is a high probability that the current 'I' will commit suicide.

Just like the depression that can be created simply

by rounding your lips.

It's a Sunday morning
yet even though there is no postman, so much news is piling up in my heart.
Who can have sent it all?

As I look at it, line by line,
your blank space,

I write a reply on it.

I am too abnormal
to admit that I'm crazy.

It's so easy to work like this.

Living in an easy way may not be the modern way of survival

but even if more and more people are taking it easy, the world is going well anyway.

I am the abundant blank space of the 21st century.

Oh,

bottomless

your quoted silence, blank space.

Since one blank space is the same as another blank space,

if I'm like you,

estimating the distance and time from one greeting to another greeting:
Hello Egoist! Hello, Transist!

You who will greet by adding suffix to prefix
there is no center, there is no essence, there is no fight,

There is only temperament.

My coordinates start here and there.
Now dispersed outside of the grandfather clock.

I don't like self-hurt or threats
so suicide is prohibited.

Loneliness being like a wolf,
once it is tamed
it becomes a peace like a dog.
It becomes peaceful like a dog,
becomes a peaceful dog.

The overdue 20th century is returned to
nobody knows how many hairs.

Or maybe

to the navel's librarian of the navel
that resembles a cave with a blocked entrance.

Smooth as a straight line

When I heard that it was snowing, I boarded a train. It was a train back home. My hometown is winter's snowy weather. Finding the climate was like a nomadic journey. What might have been their hometown? Could it have been an unremembered, unknown land where people do not remember their birth? Could it have been the land we were supposed to arrive at someday, if we walked following the map of the sky? Maybe the hometown was not a land, but a tribal people who remember both birth and growth.

The starting point of a long journey with no guarantee of return, when the wind of the change of seasons blows, a grasslands path opens in the body of livestock and walking together along that path, some die and some live, an era of tales without writing. *The place where the three hundred and sixtieth moon from now rises is your hometown. You were born when the morning star appeared in the desert night sky. You are that star's twin sister. The moon and the sun celebrated the day you were born by kissing with joy*. Equal velocity,

Maybe the story of how the sky, the earth, time and space conformed to the order of the wind was transmitted from mouth to mouth, as if yearning for a page in myth, so I miss my hometown, and when my parents die and my brother dies and goes into the heavens and becomes a star, I read their sparkling heart, sought the way back to my hometown, and compared their stories to the sand, hills, stones, and trees of the place I first returned to, filling empty memories.

From the southern region to the capital. My parents' trip will soon be a starry path. From one branch to flowerfall. My brother's journey will be along that path someday. The story of being born at dawn on a snowy day, the story of growing up with acacias, the story of catching beetles and eating them, the story of only the weather being left, erased stories. Now, my friend, we will only be able to see the shadows of old things that are losing their light in each other's mind .

The train passing through the tunnel cried like a blind camel. Wet flowers are falling to the ends of the earth *and there is no more weather today*. The train stopped at the so-called last stop, where it was cloudy but with no snow.

The sea outside the turbulent weather like a new country. White horses on the deep green sea were crashing against the breakwaters like a tribe denied entry. The roaring of the horses was cold and fierce in the snow, darkness fell, the stars struggled in the clouds. Lodgings where weary cattle were led and held. I plucked the ice-coated grass growing on my coat, fed the cattle, and checked the weather. *Tomorrow will be sunny and warm.* Tomorrow will be sunny and warm. The weather curved gently like a straight line, and snow began to fall inside my body.

Marine Snow

As soon as the first sentence of the diary was written, it disappeared. I wandered through the paper looking for the missing sentence. It was a two-lane road, and no cars were coming and no cars were going. There were no signposts and no guides. I stopped walking and looked up to see the direction the sky was unfolding. The blue sky shook like the surface of the sea. A huge shadow appeared, and then snow poured down. I walked on blindly again to avoid the snow. I saw a pension with the name Cozy written on a red signboard. As I entered the building, the owner with a long mustache said, looking at the snow on my coat.

"You met a dead whale.

The snow that falls into the sea is said to be the skin of a dead whale."

"A dead whale?" "That's what they say. There are times when we lose direction and flow into the past. It's like when a guest who hasn't even made a reservation suddenly arrives." I took the key the owner gave me and went up the stairs leading to room 302. The owner's voice came from behind me. "The stairs were made from whale ribs. That could be a joke." Turning around, I found the owner curling his **long, slender mustache** with his fingers. I tilted my head, opened the door and entered the room. I took off my wet clothes, hung them on a hanger, and took a shower. The warm, soft water pouring from the shower head spread out its fingers and traced my body. Putting a white robe on my flushed body, I lay on the bed and looked out the window. The green pine trees covered in snow looked like white whales under the snowy night sky. The whales seemed to be weeping as they looked at the morning stars in the cold night sky. I fell asleep watching the whales slowly melt away in the tears they shed. It was morning when I opened my eyes, and the white whale skin was dry on the sheet.

In the lobby was a one-legged dog, like an old sailor, warming himself by the stove. I sat on the sofa and stroked the dog's neck. The dog blinked its big eyes and turned its head to look in the direction the owner was walking. The owner, with his **long slender mustache**, placed a mug on the table and poured out coffee. The black coffee in the teacup turned white here and there, as if leaving some letters and then disappearing. "The road is blocked by snow. Don't worry too much. How could whale skin last long?" There was a terrace outside the window that the owner's smile blocked, and on the terrace was a chair where I could sit and look at the stream, covered in snow. Little by little, slowly, as I drank all the vanished letters, the snow began to melt just as the owner had said. As the snow melted, the chair bled like a man who had just fallen off a cliff. An old sailor looked at the bleeding chair and cried like a whale: "You must leave before the whales die." I took a taxi that the owner called. The taxi driver had the same mustache as the pension owner, but I couldn't decide whether to say he had grown a long, mustache, a long, thin mustache, or a thin, long mustache. "These taxi tires are made from whale tendons. That could be a joke." I ran through the paper, leaving the pension named Cozy, with the dying chair and a green pine tree from which the whale had melted, interrupted by the driver's smile. A thick dark cloud covered everything.

"A dead whale is passing by. That's what they say"

I cried like a river

Because you wanted to see the sea
I let the current go.

My body is shallow
so no matter how much I cry
I can't help but cry like a river.

Behind your back
after you went to see the sea
I finally became the sea.

Impossible Ho

Your girlfriend was not very talkative.
You said she came from the land of water,
the land where the ice melts into words.
I'm from the land of ice,
a country where flowing words are frozen.

Like freezing water, like melting ice,
you translated her and my words.
"The summer in Korea is tolerable."
"There are a lot of cool things in summer. Korea is worth living in even in winter."
"...There are many things that are warm in winter, right?"
Freezing and thawing were repeated through you.

My freezing point is her melting point,
her melting point is my freezing point,
we recognized a temperature that doesn't need a mouth.
Becoming quiet as soon as we lose respect for you and become quiet,
we planted ice seeds in water.

Trees growing fast,
as the fruit melts and flows,
trees of zero that freeze again.

You urged us to speak.
We were like silent scars to you.

We exchanged words that only you didn't know, then parted.

You called me after returning from the land of ice.
You said it was all over with her.
Unstoppable indecisiveness, a completely feminine Ho, you said.
I adjusted the frozen water's words.
A feminine Ho was impossible for you.
From that day on she turned towards me.
Ho is also impossible for you.
Because I'm freezing in her words.

The day your existence is futile

dropping below the freezing point,

I think of that day's trees.

I can't go to Korea anymore.

We cut our nails together

When I said I was going there, you said it was outside of space. I nodded at that. It was a faraway place I had never been to, so it was like outside of space. The air was hot there and water was scarce. Endless plains, old buildings covered in dust. People waited for the sun to set, just as they waited for the rain to stop at home. When the time came, the sunset was colored and people came out onto the street and walked towards the sky. There was also a rotation and the seasons changed. The stars and the moon rose, the wind blew, and white snow fell in winter. You said it was outside of space. I agreed with you. There is no reason why the inside and outside have to be different. I got a white house inside a gray building. The bathroom had a cracked bathtub, and on the living room bookshelf were books printed in foreign languages. Antique tableware in the kitchen, traces of water that seemed to have dried in the 19th century. In one of the two rooms I slept and in the other I kept a diary. You said that my long nails hurt you. When I thought of you, my nails grew fast. After sleeping, scratches remained on my forearms. I was afraid of thoughts full of you, so I cut my nails and came up with the same thoughts outside of my thoughts. I mopped the floor as if I was cutting my nails. I washed the bedding, deciphered texts, and washed the dishes. When I went out, I put my hands in my pockets, and when I met people, I hid my nails. Still, there was the same house outside the house. The same city outside the city, the same country outside the country, the same Earth outside the Earth. The place where I left the universe was also outside the universe where there was only you, and in the end, it was inside my thoughts full of you. Back here, I told you that I was still in space. You nodded and we cut our nails together.

Potato growing thick

I bought potatoes at a bargain price. I idly planted one in a left-over flower pot and covered it with soil. It was old soil. Would sprouts grow in old soil? A potato caught on the border between being planted or being buried was like a sentence that stopped yesterday. Whether it worked or not, the pause of life that invariably comes. The pages of time often become waste paper. I will know when it observes the soil. It will know whether to live or die.

Yellow flowerpot, old soil, unseen potato,
the unknown flowing into the soil

Old notebook, recycled paper, pointed nib,
letters scattered on paper,

Folded into a paper plane,
in the infinitely low, low-altitude fuselage
leave me to things like ants that go without thinking.

A few days passed while I forgot the potato after watering it. The potato grew surprisingly vigorously. Riding on a stalk of oblivion, my heart the size of a potato also sprouted. Someone must have completely forgotten me. My unknown feeling grateful for being forgotten. From potato to oblivion, from oblivion to heart, from heart to the unknown, from the unknown to writing, aimless forest growing thick, lonely living. This luxuriance of lying in a hammock seems to be the shade I will embrace.

Hello melanin

It was in front of a crosswalk. It was an outdoor art class. Me and you and the professor. The professor's face doesn't come to mind. He was someone I had never seen before. How can someone I don't know appear in my dreams? If it's impossible, he must be someone I don't remember or an illusion of someone I know. What am I doing? I was disgusted with thinking too theoretically. The professor didn't pay any attention to me. The professor seemed to want the theoretical me to step out of the practical dream. If the professor's wish comes true, what is the professor trying to do with you in my dream?

There was a huge sculpture inside the safety line.

One person was standing on both feet and staring over the crosswalk, another was standing with his knees bent while a third was standing with arms crossed. The professor who was walking around the sculpture asked you. What do you think is the difference between these two? I can't remember your answer. I only remember the reaction of the professor who was satisfied with your answer. **What do you think**? My answer was: Two feet want to cross the crossing and one foot wants to stay in front of the crossing. Then you said to me that the sculpture constituted a scene in a novel, so it should have been accompanied by a narrative and the professor scolded me, saying that he had given me a hint on what to say. From that moment on, I began to wake up from the dream. Actually, the answer I wanted to give was not the answer I gave, but the answer I didn't give. There was no difference between the two. Because of the professor's question about the difference, I was trying to say something. What difference does it make, whether on one or two feet, in front of the crossing or over the crossing? If I leave my dream, the professor will make progress with this person anyway. I finished the new answer I started in the dream outside the dream. I didn't know how far the professor had listened to me, so I didn't know what he was doing with you.

I started writing this right after I finished answering. I was hurriedly looking for a blank page in the notebook at my bedside, and I was told to gently flip through the pages so that you wouldn't wake up in class. When I brought this vaguely hastily written text to a bright place, I noticed that there were a lot of unrecognizable letters, lines filled with letters, and letters hung on lines. Turning on the computer and moving the letters from the airship to the destination, I couldn't help but wonder what kind of answer you had given the professor. I went back to bed and looked into your face. The bright smile seemed to go over the crossing with the professor.

The dream was black and white. I went to the bathroom and looked in the mirror. The part had gray hair that had never been seen before. The color was disappearing. Melanin leaving my skin... Bye, Melanin... In an instant, the professor's question flashed through my mind without context. Did the professor ask the difference between the two sculptures, or did he ask what I was? **What do you think?** I hoped that the professor crossing the road with you would be me twenty years after parting with Melanin.

Harmonious flowers

I was doing some repotting. I separated the wax plant we call Hoya and the schefflera called Hong Kong palm that I had bought and that had grown up together. Hoya was my childhood name that my father called me by, Hoya. Hong Kong palm is a palm from Hong Kong with its beautiful night views as seen by Soma*, the incarnation of loyalty. I had watered them abundantly once every two or three days and sprayed them from time to time, but they did not grow at all.

The only sign proving that plants that are not growing well
due to poor growing conditions are still alive

is withering

One stem of the Hong Kong palm had turned brown. The leaves of the Hoya, which should have been thick, were dry with no elasticity at all. It was only when I saw them dying that I became impatient and split them up. A rotten smell emerged from the dug-out soil. I called the time of death that flowed through the rotten soil a flower that blooms when dying, and moved the flowerpot to the window of my room where the morning sunlight was good. I also learned that I shouldn't be watering the Hoya so often.

Like a videotape that I had watched over and over again.

Like a videotape that had gone back to the beginning.

When he returns to my close friend's place left vacant in the evening after sunset, Hoya will curl up thick leaves like my lips and will whistle cheerfully.

When the Hong Kong palm, after growing vigorously, adorns a home-style nightscape that does not attract tourists, I will tell close friend when he returns: I didn't know Hong Kong's night view was so beautiful.**

Strip off the dead skin of waiting
like Father did.

A time for living
very harmoniously.

* Characters from the movie "A Better Tomorrow"
** Soma's lines from the movie "A Better Tomorrow."

POET´S NOTE

End

Born unfit for love,

exposed to a love the size of a palm,

the reason why this notebook suffers more than myself.

When I'm bored, even sorrow is fun,

because I am sad, pain is beautiful.

On nights when letters reject me

I fell longer than the night.

Like a snake that wants to pray but can't kneel,

like a snake that falls rather than kneels.

The end of the letters I wish I hadn't written,

traces of withered snakes.

Like untitled contents,
collection of titles without content.

Because it doesn't end well
let's not keep on to the end.

I only realized after writing it.
That that's the end,
that I am your end.

POET´S ESSAY

Phonological juice of a paragraph drunk after blending in a mixer

I went to the cafe. I sat by the window looking out. There were water droplets on the window. It was the footprints of the rain. It looks like the rain had got there before me. I gazed quietly at the traces left by the rain that I had not seen. What traces will I be, what kind of trace will be left for me, what kind of traces will I leave? A few thoughts were like fingers splitting from the palm of a hand. I looked down at my hand. It was obviously my hand, but it didn't suit me. It was like someone else's hand. It seemed for a moment that something that was not a hand had briefly got mixed up with me in the form of a hand. I lifted my head and looked out the window. There are 700-numbered buses and various private cars on the road.

Endless processions of students after school on the crosswalks. Somewhere outside the window, somewhere I couldn't see, as if there was an axis of rotation of the world, people and things were like a mixture of materials being ground in a mixer. To my right is the afterimage of the person who just left, and to my left is you reading a book. I was standing among passers-by. It may be just a touch, but it is a phenomenon that was created by pulling each other now that the attraction of the substances that had been warm in the past did not disappear, but remained together as you and me, so I fell into an illusion that we might have been mixed like this for a while. I was like a mixer, so I gathered up the thoughts that came to my mind and put them in the mixer and spun them around.

All that has disappeared is my previous life.
Because I can't remember my past life

It is a jungle where friend and foe cannot be identified.

Coming with a purified body, entangled in relationships, become bitter with resentment,

I grew dirty again.

Inside a tree, there is heartwood, in which the living cells have been destroyed.

Trees coexist with death,

the steadfast death that supports the trunk and the branches.

If I fall in love with you

your face would become my heart,

if I come to hate you

your face would be the back of my head.

You are my death.

I live with my death

All that has disappeared is my previous life.

Because I can't remember my past life

I am an island floating in a sea of oblivion.

If I wear out and sink, what will my death support?
Maybe I live with a past life I can't remember?
I am your death.
You live with me.

I look inside the mixer. Past life, death, love, hate. These are the words I see. I don't really like them, but I haven't been able to hone the sophisticated workings of the mind to replace them. So I imagine my past life and immerse myself in words such as love and hate as a result of relationship. Also, because this present life is not as enjoyable as it might be, 'If I live again from the beginning, will I be able to escape from this poem', 'If I live again from the beginning, will the result be the same?' 'If I am reborn as a human, will I be able to become a different person?' 'Or will be become myself again?' These useless thoughts are jumbled up. Being like a mixer, I spun the mixer one more time and poured the juice of a paragraph onto the paper.

All that has disappeared is my previous life Because I can't remember my past life It is a jungle where friend and foe cannot be identified Coming with a purified body, entangled in relationships, become bitter with resentment, I grew dirty again Inside a tree, there is heartwood, in which the living cells have been destroyed Trees coexist with death, the steadfast death that supports the trunk and the branches If I fall in love with you your face would become my heart, if I come to hate you your face would be the back of my head You are my death I live with my death All that has disappeared is my previous life Because I can't remember my past life I am an island floating in a sea of oblivion If I wear out and sink, what will my death support? Maybe I live with a past life I can't remember? I am your death You live with me

The juice has the same content but the line breaks have disappeared. Of course, this is an almost impossible miracle juice among the results of near-infinite phonological combinations. But I suspect that the phonemes may not have returned to where they were originally. The suspicion that the letters of 'disappeared' and of 'you' may have changed, and suspect that the vowels of 'love' and of 'hate' may have changed. So in front of you I am anxious, wondering if love is sad and sometimes turns into hate. The belief that even if I wasn't me in the past, still that was me too, and that even if I became someone other than me in the future, that would also be me, has made this juice. I look at the juice. The appearance of the phonemes that quickly adapted to the context seems perfect. With this logic, I keep imagining that a hand that belonged to someone in the past, or something that was not a hand, may now be my hand. But why do my hands always look like other people's hands? A human being is a grammatical unit that is difficult to adapt to. If you grind this juice one more time, you might end up with something like this.

Everything is your death, your floating past life. Memory cannot be reincarnated, so it is a jungle where you can't identify friend and foe. I came with a purified heart, got entangled in a body, and became worn and dirty again. It must have been a relationship filled with grudges. Living cells were wiped out from the tree inside the body. There was a strong life in the sea of heartwood and oblivion. If you love me you will live with the death that supports the trunk and branches If you hate me you will live with the death of the tree that would have been the back of my head Your face is my death .I live together with my previous life Everything that has disappeared is my island. My face is my previous life. I can't remember my past life, so what will my death support? Even if I don't remember, I will live with a certain you. It will be my sunken death.

Still needing to get used to, this juice is like my body with unsuitable hands. Could this juice be a good juice to drink in this lifetime? How many more spins will it take to turn this juice into a drinkable mixture? What was the original appearance of this juice? Was the original look beautiful? Was it really in its original form? How did I become who I am today after going through such dizzying spinning? Stop thinking and pour out the juice. After pouring, I looked and looked again, and this juice is like juice, and if I drink it like your eyebrows that may have lodged in my face, it looks drinkable as it is.

The moment I drank the juice I sank into my previous

life again, and I am in the laptops-only seat for book searches in the library. The search records left by someone on the search-only computer, the afterimages of those who left in search of documents in the library, and the scent of coffee you are drinking over there are blended with me. What were you and I in the past? How long will you and I pass by? Should this passing just end as a passing? My words that you can't hear are so much mixed with you, they jump and jump. Breathing in my face is your peaceful silence.

COMMENTARY

Time to count the wolf's teeth marks

Lim Ji-hoon (Literary Critic)

When imagining a poet writing a poem, people usually think of two things. One shows him engrossed, burying his face in the manuscript, in agony, and the other shows him writing a poem like a genius at a single stroke. However, what I came up with while reading this collection was a little different from both of those. The image that came to mind was that of a child playing with toys and creating a small world by adding his own story and setting to each toy. It was not so much the figure of a poet writing in agony, but rather closer to an innocent figure who continued to write sentences while touching each word he met by chance, talking to it, adding imagination, and sometimes erasing it.

That was probably because the charm I found in this poetry collection was similar to the charm I felt when reading short essay collections such as 'X-File', 'Fantasy Express', or the recent 'Love, Death, Robot'. Talk of different worlds that cannot be reduced to a single poetic subject, the charming and individual voices of the narrators emerging from each poem, and talk of different worlds that cannot be reduced to a single theme. Despite the common factors of fundamental discord with the world and alienation of the subject, the polyphonic voices and witty imaginings that make all these poetic movements irreducible to an asymptotic movement towards the embodiment of a specific factor are to me the essence of this collection. It was one of the driving forces that kept me reading.

In fact, the poet may not remember, but I did once meet him. When I was just starting to learn poetry, he lent me his first book of poetry and invited me to a party (embarrassingly, I haven't returned that book to him yet. He still complains that it was valuable and wants me to return it). The appearance of the poet I met at that time was similar to my imagination but a little different. Contrary to what I had imagined, I remember that he answered my trivial questions with a low voice and slight gestures. Kind and gentle, but somehow innocent, somehow made me feel he was like a little boy. I think that's probably the biggest reason I've developed a secret inner intimacy with him.

To tell the truth, I have been reading his poetry collection for a long time. However, I still have not fully grasped his poems, and each time they drive me to a new question, and a little despair. That feeling that comes from the fact that I don't have a language to describe what I like, the fascination which I feel, is also the reason I'm writing an epilogue which is not an epilogue. I often take out his collection and read it. Sometimes I read a poem seriously thinking about the poetic effect or the arrangement of images, and sometimes I read a poem as if I was watching an action play without thinking. What remains is the fact that the poems are like pictures of an incomprehensible size to me, so I had no choice but to read them as separate pieces. It's like looking at the world through a small window, imagining it, and creating your own story.... Maybe that's why I've been reading his poetry collection for a long time.

When I received and read the manuscript of this poetry collection to write an epilogue, the first emotion I felt was joy. Still, here, the polyphonic voices that cannot be reduced to one, and the various emotions and sensations that cannot be brought together by a single theme come alive as 'poems' one by one. The wolf, the different voices looking at the wolf's teeth, the person thinking about himself, someone experimenting with the devil, the 'me' who is afraid of turning into a dog, and the child sitting in the attic sadly pondering on the Jungle Book They were all fighting their own battles in the notebook. Still, each of them easily escaped my imagination, drawing unique images, and possessing a unique quality that cannot be reduced to a single voice. Sometimes the poems sounded like the voices of extremists who had disappeared beyond time, and when he whispered "Goodbye Mr. Tree" to someone who could not be termed a tree, that half-baked joke sounded like the voice of someone supremely familiar.

And it contained deepened wolf's teeth marks. Of course, this may be just my misreading, different from the poet's intention, but when I looked at the words wolf's tooth marks, I thought of that.

A notebook that has been written and erased countless times and written in again, leaving only traces like footprints on a snowy field. Maybe this statement is also like that, I don't know. I also had to write, erase, write, and erase this epilogue, leaving countless tooth marks.

When I encountered the sentence "Just as I was not born to live, but live because I was born,/ I don't need blank space to write, I need writing to fill the blank space," I also thought of that. We all have different tastes and we live our lives with our own desires, but in fact, I think that it may be nothing more than imitating the tastes and desires of others that we have been forced to adopt to fill our boring and tedious lives. In fact, I felt bankrupt as if I had been exposed to writing and erasing just pretending to have tastes and desires without any taste. On reading "Wolf, you are not the light. You are the child of a torn sound" I scratched my breastbone, wondering if there was also a wolf inside me. On reading "When the devil is busy, instead of himself/ he sends you a drink" I felt as if I had found a reason for living. What's certain is that beneath all these phrases are deep wolf-tooth marks. I read the poems slowly, feeling the teeth marks in every sentence.

Perhaps reading the poems like this is like looking at someone for a moment through a perforated sheet of paper. Without being able to see the whole, there is the appearance of getting caught up in each sentence and being engrossed in it. But I still can't fully grasp the poems, I just keep thinking about the sentences and drawing the poet's likeness. At first, I thought about inserting the picture I drew here, but somehow that seems disrespectful toward those who would like to receive this poetry collection, so I will just leave small tooth marks like this. I'm using the excuse that it's a statement rather than a commentary. Now that I think about it, I imagine that might be the only way for me to appreciate the poetry. Because it's not possible to understand every place in the world, there are landscapes that you can look at for a long time with awe and horror at the same time. And I would also like to say, as an epilogue, that people who grow up reading these poems and admiring him are still writing. "Like you, I also love myself as a plant in a wine glass."

I still don't understand the poems, I don't understand the words, but the wolves will sit here and leave their teeth marks for a long time to come. I will underline sentences that I find attractive, or leave my own interpretations, leaving new tooth marks on the page behind. Convinced that our individual questions are the only way to read these poems more deeply, I return to the first page of the collection, still thrilled by what they say, eager to read from beginning to end once again.

WHAT THEY SAY ABOUT PARK JANG-HO

K POET

Park Jang-ho's poems are light but do not fly away easily. They stay close, but are ready to move away from time to time. His language is light and his exploration is sensuous. He delves into his language, which supports his poetic ideas, in vertical and horizontal directions. The humor, wit, and innumerable latent emotions are awakened whenever a scene unfolds. He does not neglect language that does not hesitate, its free movements and poetic rifts. His narratives twist and unfold with a lightness without hesitation. Language that dances with vitality, operating in a lively manner, appears here and there.

Lee Duk-Joo, "Moments of wonder capable of being isolated," *Poetry and World* No. 54 (2016)

Whereas the utterances of lyrical poetry familiar to us are an identification and empathy that transform the unfamiliar into the familiar, transforming the unknown into the known, and empathizing with the unfamiliar, Park Jang-ho's poetry transforms the unknown into the unknown, thereby transforming the unfamiliar world. It develops in an open-ended way.

Ko Bong-Jun, "Two Possibilities of Poetic Speech,"
Quarterly Poetry No. 63 (2018)

K-POET

A Morning with only Writing Left

Written by Park Jang-ho
Translated by Brother Anthony of Taizé
Published by ASIA Publishers
Address 445, Hoedong-gil, Paju-si, Gyeonggi-do, Korea
Tel (8231).944.5058
Email bookasia@hanmail.net
Homepage Address www.bookasia.org

ISBN 979-11-5662-317-5 (set) | 979-11-5662-613-8 (04810)
First published in Korea by ASIA Publishers 2022

This book is published with the support of the Literature Translation Institute of Korea (LTI Korea).

K-Fiction series

최근에 발표된 단편소설 중 가장 우수하고 흥미로운 작품을 엄선하여 출간하는 〈K-픽션〉은 한국문학의 생생한 현장을 국내외 독자들과 실시간으로 공유하고자 기획되었습니다. 원작의 재미와 품격을 최대한 살린 〈K-픽션〉 시리즈는 매 계절마다 새로운 작품을 선보입니다.

001 버핏과의 저녁 식사-**박민규** Dinner with Buffett-**Park Min-gyu**
002 아르판-**박형서** Arpan-**Park hyoung su**
003 애드벌룬-**손보미** Hot Air Balloon-**Son Bo-mi**
004 나의 클린트 이스트우드-**오한기** My Clint Eastwood-**Oh Han-ki**
005 이베리아의 전갈-**최민우** Dishonored-**Choi Min-woo**
006 양의 미래-**황정은** Kong' s Garden-**Hwang Jung-eun**
007 대니-**윤이형** Danny-**Yun I-hyeong**
008 퇴근-**천명관** Homecoming-**Cheon Myeong-kwan**
009 옥화-**금희** Ok-hwa-**Geum Hee**
010 시차-**백수린** Time Difference-**Baik Sou linne**
011 올드 맨 리버-**이장욱** Old Man River-**Lee Jang-wook**
012 권순찬과 착한 사람들-**이기호** Kwon Sun-chan and Nice People-**Lee Ki-ho**
013 알바생 자르기-**장강명** Fired-**Chang Kangmyoung**
014 어디로 가고 싶으신가요-**김애란** Where Would You Like To Go?-**Kim Ae-ran**
015 세상에서 가장 비싼 소설-**김민정** The World' s Most Expensive Novel-**Kim Min-jung**
016 체스의 모든 것-**김금희** Everything About Chess-**Kim Keum-hee**
017 할로윈-**정한아** Halloween-**Chung Han-ah**
018 그 여름-**최은영** The Summer-**Choi Eunyoung**
019 어느 피씨주의자의 종생기-**구병모** The Story of P.C.-**Gu Byeong-mo**
020 모르는 영역-**권여선** An Unknown Realm-**Kwon Yeo-sun**
021 4월의 눈-**손원평** April Snow-**Sohn Won-pyung**
022 서우-**강화길** Seo-u-**Kang Hwa-gil**
023 가출-**조남주** Run Away-**Cho Nam-joo**
024 연애의 감정학-**백영옥** How to Break Up Like a Winner-**Baek Young-ok**
025 창모-**우다영** Chang-mo-**Woo Da-young**
026 검은 방-**정지아** The Black Room-**Jeong Ji-a**
027 도쿄의 마야-**장류진** Maya in Tokyo-**Jang Ryu-jin**
028 홀리데이 홈-**편혜영** Holiday Home-**Pyun Hye-young**
029 해피 투게더-**서장원** Happy Together-**Seo Jang-won**
030 골드러시-**서수진** Gold Rush-**Seo Su-jin**
031 당신이 보고 싶어하는 세상-**장강명** The World You Want to See-**Chang Kang-Myoung**

바이링궐 에디션 한국 대표 소설 목록

001 **병신과 머저리** 이청준 / 제니퍼 리
002 **어둠의 혼** 김원일 / 손석주, 캐서린 로즈 토레스
003 **순이삼촌** 현기영 / 이정희
004 **엄마의 말뚝 1** 박완서 / 유영난
005 **유형의 땅** 조정래 / 전경자
006 **무진기행** 김승옥 / 케빈 오룩
007 **삼포 가는 길** 황석영/ 김우창
008 **아홉 켤레의 구두로 남은 사내** 윤흥길 / 브루스 풀턴, 주찬 풀턴
009 **돌아온 우리의 친구** 신상웅 / 손석주, 캐서린 로즈 토레스
010 **원미동 시인** 양귀자 / 전미세리
011 **중국인 거리** 오정희 / 주찬 풀턴, 브루스 풀턴
012 **풍금이 있던 자리** 신경숙 / 아그니타 테넌트
013 **하나코는 없다** 최윤 / 주찬 풀턴, 브루스 풀턴
014 **인간에 대한 예의** 공지영 / 주찬 풀턴, 브루스 풀턴
015 **빈처** 은희경 / 전승희
016 **필론의 돼지** 이문열 / 제이미 챙
017 **슬로우 불릿** 이대환 / 전승희
018 **직선과 독가스** 임철우 / 크리스 최
019 **깃발** 홍희담 / 전승희
020 **새벽 출정** 방현석 / 주다희, 안선재
021 **별을 사랑하는 마음으로** 윤후명 / 전미세리
022 **목련공원** 이승우 / 유진 라르센-할록
023 **칼에 찔린 자국** 김인숙 / 손석주, 캐서린 로즈 토레스
024 **회복하는 인간** 한강 / 전승희
025 **트렁크** 정이현 / 브루스 풀턴, 주찬 풀턴
026 **판문점** 이호철 / 테오도르 휴즈
027 **수난 이대** 하근찬 / 케빈 오룩
028 **분지** 남정현 / 전승희
029 **봄 실상사** 정도상 / 전승희
030 **은행나무 사랑** 김하기 / 손석주, 캐서린 로즈 토레스
031 **눈사람 속의 검은 항아리** 김소진 / 크리스 최
032 **오후, 가로지르다** 하성란 / 전승희
033 **나는 봉천동에 산다** 조경란 / 쉥크 카리
034 **그렇습니까? 기린입니다** 박민규 / 김소라
035 **성탄특선** 김애란 / 제이미 챙
036 **무자년의 가을 사흘** 서정인 / 제이미 챙
037 **유자소전** 이문구 / 제이미 챙
038 **향기로운 우물 이야기** 박범신 / 마야 웨스트
039 **월행** 송기원 / 제인 리
040 **협죽도 그늘 아래** 성석제 / 전승희
041 **아겔다마** 박상륭 / 전승희
042 **내 영혼의 우물** 최인석 / 전승희
043 **당신에 대해서** 이인성 / 마야 웨스트
044 **회색 시** 배수아 / 장정화, 앤드류 제임스 키스트
045 **브라운 부인** 정영문 / 정영문
046 **속옷** 김남일 / 전승희
047 **상하이에 두고 온 사람들** 공선옥 / 전승희
048 **모두에게 복된 새해** 김연수 / 마야 웨스트
049 **코끼리** 김재영 / 미셸 주은 김
050 **먼지별** 이경 / 전미세리
051 **혜자의 눈꽃** 천승세 / 전승희
052 **아베의 가족** 전상국 / 손석주
053 **문 앞에서** 이동화 / 전미세리
054 **그리고, 축제** 이혜경 / 브루스 풀턴, 주찬 풀턴
055 **봄밤** 권여선 / 전승희
083 **상춘곡** 윤대녕 / 테레사 김

056 **오늘의 운세** 한창훈 / 케롱 린

057 **새** 전성태 / 전승희

058 **밀수록 다시 가까워지는** 이기호 / 테레사 김

059 **유리방패** 김중혁 / 케빈 오록

060 **전당포를 찾아서** 김종광 / 손석주

061 **도둑견습** 김주영 / 손석주

062 **사랑하라, 희망 없이** 윤영수 / 전승희

063 **봄날 오후, 과부 셋** 정지아 / 브랜든 맥케일, 김윤경

064 **유턴 지점에 보물지도를 묻다** 윤성희 / 이지은

065 **쁘이거나 쯔이거나** 백가흠 / 장정화, 앤드류 제임스 키스트

066 **나는 음식이다** 오수연 / 크리스 최

067 **트럭** 강영숙 / 전승희

068 **통조림 공장** 편혜영 / 미셸 주은 김

069 **꽃** 부희령 / 리처드 해리스, 김현경

070 **피의일요일** 윤이형 / 전승희

071 **북소리** 송영 / 손석주

072 **발칸의 장미를 내게 주었네** 정미경 / 스텔라 김

073 **아무도 돌아오지 않는 밤** 김숨 / 전미세리

074 **젓가락여자** 천운영 / 전미세리

075 **아직 일어나지 않은 일** 김미월 / 전미세리

076 **언니를 놓치다** 이경자 / 장정화, 앤드류 키스트

077 **아들** 윤정모 / 쉥크 카리

078 **명두** 구효서 / 미셸 주은 김

079 **모독** 조세희 / 손석주

080 **화요일의 강** 손홍규 / 제이미 챙

081 **고수** 이외수 / 손석주

082 **말을 찾아서** 이순원 / 미셸 주은 김

084 **삭매와 자미** 김별아 / 전미세리

085 **저만치 혼자서** 김훈 / 크리스 최

086 **감자** 김동인 / 케빈 오록

087 **운수 좋은 날** 현진건 / 케빈 오록

088 **탈출기** 최서해 / 박선영

089 **과도기** 한설야 / 전승희

090 **지하촌** 강경애 / 서지문

091 **날개** 이상 / 케빈 오록

092 **김 강사와 T 교수** 유진오 / 손석주

093 **소설가 구보씨의 일일** 박태원 / 박선영

094 **비 오는 길** 최명익 / 자넷 풀

095 **빛 속에** 김사량 / 크리스토퍼 스캇

096 **봄 · 봄** 김유정 / 전승희

097 **벙어리 삼룡이** 나도향 / 박선영

098 **달밤** 이태준 / 김종운, 브루스 풀턴

099 **사랑손님과 어머니** 주요섭 / 김종운, 브루스 풀턴

100 **갯마을** 오영수 / 마샬 필

101 **소망** 채만식 / 브루스 풀턴, 주찬 풀턴

102 **두 파산** 염상섭 / 손석주

103 **풀잎** 이효석 / 브루스 풀턴, 주찬 풀턴

104 **맥** 김남천 / 박선영

105 **꺼삐딴 리** 전광용 / 마샬 필

106 **소나기** 황순원 / 에드워드 포이트라스

107 **등신불** 김동리 / 설순봉

108 **요한 시집** 장용학 / 케빈 오록

109 **비 오는 날** 손창섭 / 전승희

110 **오발탄** 이범선 / 마샬 필